My First Adventures

MY FIRST TRIP TO THE
DOCTOR

By Katie Kawa

Gareth Stevens
Publishing

Please visit our website, www.garethstevens.com. For a free color catalog of all our high-quality books, call toll free 1-800-542-2595 or fax 1-877-542-2596.

Library of Congress Cataloging-in-Publication Data

Kawa, Katie.
My first trip to the doctor / Katie Kawa.
    p. cm. — (My first adventures)
Includes index.
ISBN 978-1-4339-6247-9 (pbk.)
ISBN 978-1-4339-6248-6 (6-pack)
ISBN 978-1-4339-6245-5 (library binding)
1. Children—Medical examinations—Juvenile literature. 2. Children—Preparation for medical care—Juvenile literature. I. Title.
RJ50.5.K39 2012
618.92'0075—dc23

2011016966

First Edition

Published in 2012 by
Gareth Stevens Publishing
111 East 14th Street, Suite 349
New York, NY 10003

Editor: Katie Kawa
Designer: Haley W. Harasymiw

All illustrations by Planman Technologies

Printed in the United States of America

CPSIA compliance information: Batch #CW12GS: For further information contact Gareth Stevens, New York, New York at 1-800-542-2595.

Contents

Time for a Checkup 4

I'm Growing! 10

What Doctors Do 14

Words to Know 24

Index. 24

Today, I am going to the doctor.

My dad is taking me
for a checkup.
The doctor makes sure
I am healthy.

I need a checkup
one time every year.

A nurse helps the doctor.
She sees how tall I am.

I stand on a scale.
It shows how much I weigh.

13

Then, the doctor comes in.
He has a white coat.

He listens to my heart.

He looks at my eyes,
ears, and nose.
He uses a small light.

He looks in my mouth too.
I have to open it wide.

My doctor says
I am very healthy!

Musculoskeletal System

Words to Know

coat

nurse

scale

Index

checkup 6, 8   nurse 10

healthy 6, 22   scale 12